THE FIGHT FOR
IRAQ

CREDITS

EDITOR   Major Angus Beaton RLC Media Operations Group (V)

IMAGES   Major Angus Beaton RLC Media Operations Group (V)
Warrant Officer Class 2 Giles Penfound RLC
Staff Sergeant Chris Andrew RLC (Mobilised Regular Reserve)
Sergeant Stu McKenzie RLC
Corporal Paul Jarvis RLC
Corporal Dave Liddle RLC

WORDS   Major Peter Caddick-Adams TD RMLY Media Operations Group (V)
Graham Thomas GICS

DESIGN   Major Lynda Black RRF Media Operations Group (V)
Major John Skliros TD RGJ (V)

ACKNOWLEDGEMENTS

The Editor would like to thank the following people who lent their advice or expertise during the compiling of The Fight for Iraq and without whom this book would have been incomplete.

The staff of the Army Medal Office, Droitwich
Lieutenant Colonel Sally Cadec, MoD (Honours & Awards)
Terry Champion, Army Picture Desk
David Collett, HQ ATRA
John Easterby, Independent Photographers Group
John Elliott, Soldier Magazine
Steve Lane, Army Casualty Records Branch
Nigel Oak, HQ Land Command
Air Commodore (Retd.) Graham Pitchfork MBE FRAeS
Captain Tom Wilson-Hutton-Stott RGBW

THE FIGHT FOR
IRAQ

FOREWORD

GENERAL SIR MIKE JACKSON KCB CBE DSO ADC Gen

CHIEF OF THE GENERAL STAFF

The Fight for Iraq tells the British Army's story of the first six months of Operation Telic. In that short time, almost a third of the Army, servicemen and women, regulars and reservists, deployed to the Gulf, fought a war to liberate Iraq, and began the longer process of building the peace for the benefit of the Iraqi people. This was, and continues to be, a remarkable achievement. The Army at its best, and a testament to our training and professionalism.

This book covers specifically the British Army's contribution to the liberation of Iraq, although it is important to remember that this was a joint operation involving the Royal Navy and the Royal Air Force, and it was also a coalition involving other nations, most notably the US and Australia. During the war the 1st (UK) Armoured Division was under command of the US 1st Marine Expeditionary Force and we continue to operate closely with our US allies. More recently, the coalition has expanded to include many other nations, with the UK-led Multinational Division in South Eastern Iraq comprising troops from Italy, Norway, Romania, Denmark, the Netherlands, the Czech Republic, Portugal, Lithuania, New Zealand and Japan.

The British Army called up nearly 5,000 Territorial Army and regular reservists in the early days of Operation Telic, the largest number since the Suez crisis in 1956. Few of the photographs in this book will identify these part-time professional soldiers, because once mobilised they quickly became part of a single war-winning team: indistinguishable from their regular counterparts. Their contribution was immense. Quite simply, we could not have achieved the success we did without them; we are greatly indebted to their families and employers whose consistent and essential support was impressive throughout — and continues so to be.

Although this book focuses solely on the British Army's deployed operation in Kuwait and Iraq, there were many other Army personnel serving in the UK, in Cyprus, Germany and elsewhere, including families, who supported the front line in the Gulf. Without them, it would have been impossible to mount and sustain an operation on the scale of Operation Telic.

The following photographs record some of the extraordinary events that took place during the operation to liberate Iraq. This book illustrates the professionalism, fortitude and courage of those Army personnel who were there. Above all, it is a tribute to those who fought and lost their lives.

For many, Operation Telic was to be their first experience of desert warfare.

Field training and practising drills was to occupy much of the assembling force's time.

CONTENTS

INTRODUCTION

THE INTERVENTION of coalition military forces in March 2003 brought to an end a brutal regime that began with Saddam Hussein's seizing power in 1979. Iraq under Saddam invaded Iran in September 1980 and Kuwait in August 1990, and the Iraqi people had suffered greatly throughout Saddam's rule. His use of chemical weapons in Iran and against his Kurdish subjects proved his determination to remain in power.

Following the end of the first Gulf War in 1991, with Kuwait's sovereignty restored by the US-led coalition, restrictions were placed on Iraq's military deployments. Two no-fly zones were imposed in northern and southern Iraq, and a programme was initiated by the UN Special Commission (UNSCOM) to monitor Iraq's military arsenals. This encountered increasing obstruction from the Iraqi authorities, leading finally to the withdrawal of the UN inspectors in December 1998.

In November 2002, the UN declared it would no longer tolerate Iraq's defiance of international law. UN Security Council Resolution (UNSCR) 1441 was unanimously adopted, declaring Iraq in material breach of previous resolutions, and setting out new procedures for inspections, together with the threat of serious consequences in the event of non-cooperation. This was a final opportunity for Iraq to comply, and UN Monitoring, Verification and Inspection Commission (UNMOVIC) inspectors were allowed back later that month. However, it soon became clear that Iraq was failing to offer active cooperation.

Prudent military planning had already begun, because contingencies had to be in place if diplomacy failed. These preparations strengthened diplomatic efforts by demonstrating resolve, and further delays

would have given Saddam's regime more time to prepare for war against his neighbours or coalition forces in the region.

The UK now joined a US-led coalition prepared, if necessary, to use force to secure Iraqi compliance. The UK Government's political objective was to disarm Saddam of his weapons of mass destruction that threatened his neighbours and his people. It also undertook to support the Iraqi people's desire for peace, prosperity, and freedom. The Government was also determined that, if military action was necessary, civilian casualties and damage to the economic infrastructure would be kept to the minimum, and emergency humanitarian relief provided where necessary.

Iraq was already an operational theatre, with US and UK aircraft enforcing the no-fly zones. In late November 2002 the Defence Secretary announced that an initial assessment of the possible requirement for reservists was being made. The need for additional military equipment and specific modifications was also reviewed, a process announced in Parliament on 25th November. Further preparations included approaching the shipping market in mid-December to tender for transportation vessels, and improving the readiness of troops by undertaking specific training and reducing the notice to move of some units.

Overall planning for the operation was led by the United States but the UK was kept fully involved by having key personnel embedded in US Central Command in Tampa and elsewhere. Since the diplomatic process continued, it was impossible to know whether or when operations might be required. Nevertheless, the outline plan remained consistent. The focus was on mounting a rapid, synchronised and precise campaign to over-

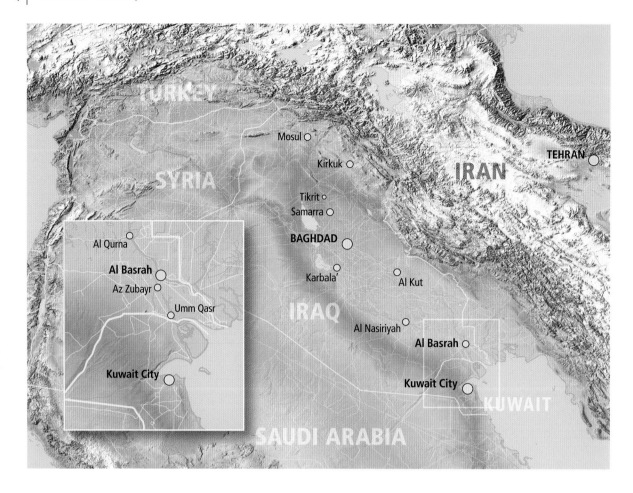

whelm Saddam Hussein's regime and security forces, while minimising the risk of civilian casualties or damage to Iraq's essential services. The aim was to prevent Saddam from putting into effect his most destructive options, such as using weapons of mass destruction, destroying civil infrastructure or creating humanitarian or environmental catastrophes, as he had done in Kuwait when he withdrew Iraqi forces in 1991.

As planning developed, the Government sought to provide a balanced contribution to coalition forces, capable of playing a major role in any operation. Initial plans envisaged UK and US land and air forces operating from the north and deploying through Turkey as well as from Kuwait in the south. In the event, the Turkish Government was unable to secure parliamentary approval for such deployments. The planning option was thus confined to Kuwait, with UK ground forces expected to play a key role in southern Iraq, enabling US forces to advance rapidly to the north.

On 24th February, the UK, the US and Spain tabled a draft resolution, making it clear that Iraq had failed to take the opportunity provided in UNSCR 1441. Despite significant diplomatic efforts, it was reluctantly concluded that a Security Council consensus on this new resolution would not be possible. Faced with continu-

ing Iraqi intransigence, coalition forces commenced military operations on 20th March 2003.

In the pages that follow, *The Fight For Iraq* chronicles the military build-up to war, the war-fighting phase, and the immediate aftermath. With the collapse of the regime in April 2003, coalition forces began the next phase of their mission, working closely with the Iraqi people to help create the foundations of a secure and stable environment.

The Fight For Iraq ends its story in June 2003, although much has been achieved since then. The coalition in Iraq has become increasingly multinational: the UK-led Multinational Division (South East) includes troops from Italy, Norway, Romania, Denmark, the Netherlands, the Czech Republic, Portugal, Lithuania, New Zealand and Japan. Commerce has returned to the streets of Basrah. Electricity and clean water now flow freely on demand. Hospitals and medical facilities are available for those who need them. Civic structures have been established, as has a new Iraqi Army and Police Force. The Iraqi people can now look forward to gaining control of both their sovereignty and their destiny. They have been given a new beginning, due, in part, to the efforts and sacrifices of those depicted in the pages of this book.

Men of the 1st Battalion, The Royal Regiment of Fusiliers prepare to
clear a dummy trench during the build-up training in Kuwait.

THE GATHERING
STORM

As a result of the worsening situation in the Gulf, and continued Iraqi failure to cooperate with the international community, the UK first announced the formation of a maritime task force on 7th January 2003. This included a large proportion of 3 Commando Brigade, and represented the largest amphibious force deployed since 1982. Not long after, a sizeable ground force element was also deployed, built around the 1st (UK) Armoured Division.

The Defence Secretary announced on 20th January that the Army's contribution, drawn from units based in Germany and the UK, would include 16 Air Assault Brigade, which would provide a substantial proportion of the coalition's air assault capability, and 7th Armoured Brigade, making this the largest land force commitment overseas since the Gulf War of 1991.

On 6th February, it was announced that the Royal Air Force's presence in the region would be increased from 25 to 100 aircraft. Overall, the UK contribution to coalition forces in the Gulf would amount eventually to ten per cent of the total of 467,000 personnel, mostly American, but including an Australian contingent of 4,000.

The UK's military build-up in the Gulf was rapid and initially restrained in the hope that the crisis would be resolved by diplomacy rather than force. Once a military option looked more likely for the UK, the pressure was on to deploy a force of 46,000 men and women and their equipment to the Gulf region — a journey for some of more than 3,400 miles. A similar UK force had in 1991 been moved to the region in 22 weeks ready for the first Gulf War. In 2003, this Herculean task was achieved in just ten weeks. More than 28,000 Regular and Reserve Army personnel were moved to the Gulf.

The Territorial Army's 165 Port and Maritime Regiment, Royal Logistic Corps (Volunteer) was the first volunteer regiment to be mobilised since the Second World War and shadowed its Regular counterpart, 17 Port and Maritime Regiment, Royal Logistic Corps (RLC), in loading equipment — including more than 2,000 vehicles — and supplies on to 62 ships in the UK and Germany, and unloading them in the Gulf.

As Army units arrived in the desert, they were put through realistic training packages while they acclimatised and prepared their equipment for war in a hot and challenging environment. Soldiers rehearsed their missions in chemical warfare suits while, in spare moments, they wrote letters or electronic mail dubbed 'e-blueys'.

Huge tented camps were established in the Kuwaiti desert for US and UK forces. Feeding such vast numbers of troops, keeping them supplied with water, training ammunition, issuing desert clothing and equipment, and meeting health and hygiene requirements — all within range of Iraqi missiles — presented an unprecedented logistical burden. Members of every RLC regiment contributed in some way to meeting this challenge. Much, of course, relied on the ability of logisticians in the UK to dispatch equipment as it was required, anticipate other needs, and source urgent requirements as they arose.

By 18th March, the three coalition partners had assembled and trained a huge fighting force, while their

Royal Air Force and civilian chartered aircraft were used
to fly troops to Kuwait from Germany and the UK.

governments had concluded that the diplomatic options
were almost exhausted. A final ultimatum was issued
for Saddam Hussein to leave Iraq, which expired in the
early hours of 20th March. Having worked often with
our US coalition partners, the British force was placed
under command of the American Central Command
(CENTCOM), headed by US General Tommy Franks.

The British National Contingent Commander, Air
Marshal Brian Burridge — the senior British officer in
the region — was based in Qatar with the 500-strong
National Contingent Headquarters (NCHQ). Waiting
in the Kuwaiti desert lay 1st (UK) Armoured Division,
with the US 15th Marine Expeditionary Unit (15 MEU)
under command.

Finally, in order to record the first major war of the
21st century, more than 700 journalists were embedded
with many coalition units at every level.

Right and opposite: Soldiers from 7th Armoured Brigade
(The Desert Rats) say farewell to their families as they prepare
to leave their base at Bergen-Hohne in Germany.

More than 600 armoured fighting vehicles were brought ashore in Kuwait under
the watchful eye of the men and women of the Port and Maritime Regiments.

Men of 17 Port and Maritime Regiment, Royal Logistic Corps, ferry port operators
to the container ships in an Army work boat at the naval base in Kuwait.

The tailoress at HQ 7th Armoured Brigade sewed the unit's insignia
on to more than 1,200 newly-issued desert uniforms.

Members of 33 Field Hospital, Royal Army Medical Corps,
assemble their tented hospital in the Kuwait desert.

On arrival, all personnel completed a detailed registration process. Pay, medical and personal details had to be checked before they could go on to join their units.

The desert conditions were a real challenge for catering staff. Based on experience gained in previous campaigns and recent desert-based training exercises, units in the forward areas were fed from central kitchens run by the Royal Logistic Corps.

British personnel arriving in Kuwait underwent a detailed induction process which included briefings on road regulations, local customs and laws, health matters and security.

Vehicles off-loaded from military and chartered merchant ships at the port of Kuwait
were gathered on the dockside and moved in convoys to logistic and front-line units.

Many thousands of litres of fuel a day were required
to keep the force's vehicles on the move.

Both day and night, the heavy-lift capability of Chinook helicopters of the Joint Helicopter Force
provided swift delivery of stores, equipment and troops throughout the assembling force.

Desert winds could quickly whip the fine sand into a blinding mist. Issued
goggles and shemaghs or face scarves were standard wear for everyone.

Test-firing weapon systems in desert conditions provided troops with valuable practice and experience. The MILAN Platoon of The 1st Battalion, The Royal Irish Regiment fire their vehicle-mounted anti-tank missiles.

The prospect of having to use their professional skills added a
special edge to the training for soldiers of the force.

Troops were quick to adapt to desert living and
improvise where the luxuries of home were limited.

Whether firing artillery, clearing a trench, camouflaging vehicles or
patrolling in the desert, all were focused on what might be ahead.

With the flat, hard-packed sand offering little shelter or protection against gunfire and exploding artillery shells,
staff from 7 Armoured Brigade HQ dig trenches for an overnight halt during training exercises in Kuwait.

Regular Nuclear Biological and Chemical warfare exercises and alerts ensured
troops could carry out all routine tasks as normal, both on and off duty.

Above and overleaf: Determined to maintain regimental tradition, both the 1st Battalion, Irish Guards and 1st Battalion, The Royal Irish Regiment celebrated 17th March, St Patrick's Day, in the Kuwaiti desert with parades, prayers and the presentation of lush green shamrock.

No amount of weaponry or scientific advancement can in any way deflect from the reality that it is the people who do it, and the people who make it happen. The great talent we have got is that we have people who can think for themselves, identify problems and sort them out. Man-for-man, our people are head and shoulders above most other armies. The most important thing I'll always remember about Op Telic is the people.

BRIGADIER SHAUN COWLAM, COMMANDER, 102 LOGISTIC BRIGADE

Quiet moments in March were rare but there was always time for Sunday church parade.

The padre of The 1st Battalion, The Black Watch takes communion with members of the unit.

CLOSING WITH THE
ENEMY

WITHIN THE BRITISH FORCE, 7th Armoured Brigade had also fought in the first Gulf War of 1991. The major surprise of that conflict was the destruction of the Kuwaiti oilfields by Saddam's forces as they retreated.

The chief concern for coalition planners in 2003 was that Saddam might try the same tactic on his own Al Rumaylah oilfield near the Kuwaiti border. With well-laid explosives, the regime could turn some, or all, of the 454 active oil wells into flaming torches, blackening the skies for months and polluting land and oceans far away. Oil might enter the Tigris and Euphrates rivers and reach the waters of the Persian Gulf. Oil gushing under pressure from punctured pipelines could easily delay advancing coalition forces, and Iraq's potential revenue from that oil would be wasted if this nightmare scenario were allowed to happen.

Considerable thought was given as to how to seize the twelve gas-oil separation plants and various pumping stations within the Al Rumaylah field. Although their capture was assigned to the US Marines of Regimental Combat Team 7, they were accompanied by specialists from the Royal Engineers Military Works Force, which is expert in oilfield technology, as well as members of the Joint Explosive Ordnance Disposal Group, which is trained in making-safe sabotaged or booby-trapped oil installations.

The campaign opened with air attacks on key regime targets, including Saddam Hussein himself, and there was a general expectation that there would be days, or weeks, of air strikes pounding Iraq before coalition ground forces attacked. Many former officers

and analysts were seen on television advocating this approach, which was used in 1991.

But this time the plan was to attack by land and air almost simultaneously, hoping to catch the Iraqis off-guard and increasing the likelihood that the oilfields could be seized intact. The air campaign was launched ninety minutes after the expiry of the ultimatum, in the early hours of 20th March, by coalition aircraft, including the Royal Air Force, and warships, among them two Royal Navy submarines firing Tomahawk land attack missiles.

As cruise missiles and smart bombs hit Baghdad, and Royal Marines seized several offshore objectives, reports trickled in that a few oil wells were burning. The decision was taken to commit the ground force ahead of schedule to prevent the whole Al Rumaylah field from going up in flames. The campaign plan, in simple terms, was a two-pronged attack, with US V Corps on the left thrusting north and, on the right, the US 1st Marine Expeditionary Force (1 MEF) moving on a parallel axis sixty to one hundred kilometres away.

Both US formations were Baghdad-bound, while the 1st (UK) Armoured Division — under the command of 1 MEF — was to secure a chunk of southern Iraq, centred on Basrah, Iraq's second city. 3 Commando Brigade, a key element of the British Division, in a mission rehearsed extensively, attacked the Al Faw peninsula on the night of 20th-21st March, seized gas-oil platforms, then moved up the peninsula in appalling weather. US Marines under British command fought their way into Umm Qasr port at the same time and,

The commanding officer of the 1st Battalion, The Royal Regiment of Fusiliers, addresses his men before
they move off to 'Barnsley' — the codename for 7th Armoured Brigade's forward assembly area.

throughout 21st March, the British Division poured
over the Kuwaiti border into southern Iraq. Captain
Liam Wilson, in the Royal Regiment of Fusiliers battlegroup, remembered moving forward cautiously while
coalition artillery tore through the air over his head.
Up in front, his platoon crossed the berms (artificially-
created sandbanks) that marked the frontier. "We were
the forward platoon of the entire Brigade. There was
nothing between us and the enemy."

By late afternoon on 21st March, the US Marines
had seized the key infrastructure of the Al Rumaylah
field and the British specialists were making the installations safe. Battlegroups of 7th Armoured Brigade,
which had crossed their line of departure early that
morning, acted as a flank guard for the Marines and
the Division's other formation, 16 Air Assault Brigade.

Deploying commando, armoured and air assault
brigades gave the British Divisional Commander,
Major General Robin Brims, a wide variety of options
in fighting the campaign against an unpredictable and
determined enemy. Phoenix unmanned aerial reconnaissance vehicles, launched by 32nd Regiment, Royal

Artillery, over-flew enemy territory capturing images
of enemy positions and activity providing invaluable
intelligence to coalition forces.

7th Armoured Brigade was built around two
armoured regiments, with 120 Challenger 2 tanks
(The Royal Scots Dragoon Guards and 2nd Royal Tank
Regiment) and two infantry battalions (1st Battalion,
The Black Watch and 1st Battalion, The Royal Regiment
of Fusiliers) mounted in 150 Warrior infantry fighting
vehicles and comprising about 3,400 combat troops.
Infantry companies and tank squadrons were mixed to
form combined arms battlegroups with AS90 artillery
batteries (from 3rd Regiment, Royal Horse Artillery)
and armoured engineer squadrons. Many more units
were under direct divisional command, including an
additional infantry battalion (1st Battalion, The Duke
of Wellington's Regiment) for prisoner-of-war han-
dling duties.

16 Air Assault Brigade was entirely different in com-
position, formed around 3 Regiment, Army Air Corps
and three infantry battalions (1st and 3rd Battalions,
The Parachute Regiment and 1st Battalion, The Royal

Above and overleaf: Lieutenant General James T. Conway, Commanding General, 1st US
Marine Expeditionary Force, addresses soldiers from 1st (UK) Armoured Division.

We go to liberate them, not to conquer. We will not fly our flags in their country. We are entering Iraq to free a people and the only flag that will be shown in that ancient land is their own. Show respect for them. There are some who are alive at this moment who will not be alive shortly. Those who do not wish to go on that journey, we will not send. But if you are ferocious in battle, remember to be magnanimous in victory. It is a big step to take another human life. It is not to be done lightly.

LIEUTENANT COLONEL TIM COLLINS

COMMANDING OFFICER, 1ST BATTALION, THE ROYAL IRISH REGIMENT

Damaged oil pipelines and pumping plants were quick to catch fire, generating
huge black clouds of smoke and reducing the day to an eerie half-light.

Once 26 and 39 Squadrons of 32 Armoured Engineer Regiment had breached the berm
and bridged the anti-tank ditch, convoys of armoured vehicles crossed in a constant flow.

Irish Regiment). Its artillery (7th Parachute Regiment, Royal Horse Artillery); armoured reconnaissance (The Household Cavalry Regiment); sappers (23 Regiment Royal Engineers (RE)); logistics (13 Air Assault Regiment RLC); and mechanical engineers (7 Air Assault Battalion, Royal Electrical and Mechanical Engineers (REME) were all trained to operate in the air assault role. This made it a highly flexible, manoeuvra-ble formation, capable of adapting to a wide variety of roles. It totalled about 2,500 combat troops.

The abilities of each formation complemented the others and were, in turn, sustained by 102 Logistic Brigade, with a wide variety of RLC, REME, RE, Royal Signals, Army Medical Services (including 33, 34 and 202 Field Hospitals) and Royal Military Police units under command.

The artillery was very loud and got the adrenaline flowing. We sprinted out of the back of the vehicle. It was almost comical — we were so psyched up, nothing was going to stand in our way but we couldn't get up the berm. Every six steps up the soft sand was followed by four steps back down again — not like the hard sand we'd trained on.
We were racing to the top to be the first into Iraq but were going nowhere.

LANCE CORPORAL CARDWELL,

THE ROYAL REGIMENT OF FUSILIERS

Sudden torrential downpours of rain provided a welcome cooling break for those exposed to them.

Unfortunately, the sand turned to a soggy mess that stuck to every piece of equipment.

The night of 23rd March was to be the longest night of my life. We were to give local protection for the tanks of 3rd Troop [Queen's Royal Lancers] on raids into Basrah up the main highway. The raid was going well, with five Iraqi T55 tanks being destroyed when, on the withdrawal, the British tanks received incoming rocket-propelled grenade (RPG) fire. Within seconds, Fusilier Harris had identified the RPG man and fired at him. His tracer allowed the rest of the platoon to identify this pocket of enemy and destroy them.

With all this excitement dealt with, we returned to our positions to overwatch on the bridge.
It was at this point that we were informed that twenty T72 Iraqi tanks were inbound to our
location. The officer in command of 3rd Troop stated that our odds weren't good if the T72s
were equipped with a thermal imaging capability. Never before have I felt so pleased to see
the Black Watch approaching.

LIEUTENANT CHRIS REES-GAY, PLATOON COMMANDER, THE ROYAL REGIMENT OF FUSILIERS

As advancing troops discovered abandoned or stockpiled Iraqi munitions, the Joint Explosive Ordnance Disposal Unit would be advised. Every find was assessed and — where practical — made safe or destroyed.

When we crossed the border there was an Iraqi division to our right. The intensity of the attack on them from ground force, artillery and air was ferocious. The division evaporated. Some of them surrendered but most of them scarpered. They couldn't capitulate because they had regime diehards controlling them. They actually had somebody putting a gun to their heads making commands.

MAJOR GENERAL ROBIN BRIMS

COMMANDER, 1ST (UK) ARMOURED DIVISION

The evening of 22nd March saw The Black Watch battlegroup linking up with troops from the US 1 MEF near
Az Zubayr. As they handed over their positions the Marines moved out on their way north to Baghdad.

Iraqi barracks and military camps were littered with stockpiled equipment, much of which was broken or unserviceable.

British troops seized a food aid storage compound from the enemy. The facility was then used as an operating base by troops from the Fusilier battlegroup and became known as 'The Bread Basket'.

Brigadier Graham Binns [left], commanding the 7th Armoured Brigade (The Desert Rats)
briefs Major General Robin Brims on the prevailing battle picture.

Up-armoured and modified for desert conditions, the Challenger 2 main battle
tank won its spurs in terms of mobility, survivability and firepower.

By using helicopters to spot and accurately locate damaged and burning pipelines, coalition forces helped the oil companies and
local contractors extinguish the fires. Work could then begin on repairing and restoring the flow of oil across the country.

Enemy prisoners of war were gathered in holding areas awaiting
transport to centralised coalition camps near Umm Qasr.

A sergeant major from The Royal Irish Regiment gives the signal
for his troops to start feeding Iraqi prisoners in his charge.

FOOTHOLD IN
AZ ZUBAYR

WITH UMM QASR secured by Royal Marines and US Marines, the main US forces thrust north, leaving 1st (UK) Armoured Division to shadow the American formations and attend to Basrah. Early skirmishes with Iraqi units seemed to indicate that their military cohesion was breaking down. Officers fled, leaving reluctant conscripts to fight on.

It was soon found, however, that what remained of the Iraqi military was being compelled to fight by Saddam's Ba'ath party militia. Sometimes referred to as Fedayeen, these fanatics had minimal military training and their choice of weapons — rocket-propelled grenade anti-tank weapons and AK-47 assault rifles — was as simple as their tactics. Where larger weapons were used, such as the few attacks by Iraqi tanks, there was little evidence of coordination and they were soon broken up and destroyed by British and American troops.

By 22nd March, the British Division had relieved the 1st US Marine Division, allowing it to chase north, and 7th Armoured Brigade was moving around the outskirts of Basrah. At first, taking Basrah itself was not part of the plan, but it was soon clear that the city would have to fall if the coalition was to achieve its objectives. These were to overcome Iraqi military resistance, and provide a secure environment so that normal life and civil liberty could return as quickly as possible for the Iraqi people.

This meant removing Saddam's regime, then supporting the international civilian agencies that would arrive to provide and distribute humanitarian aid, and rebuild the country's neglected and damaged infrastructure.

Once the city was identified as an objective, Major General Brims recalled: "If we had gone into Basrah in force, we would have inflicted and taken huge numbers of casualties. I was not going to have a Grozny or a Stalingrad."

Thus, 1st Armoured Division gradually dominated the terrain around Basrah without entering the city. Major Johnny Biggart, of The Royal Scots Dragoon Guards, recounted: "On the night of 22nd March, we were sent north of Basrah to stop Iraqi armoured divisions from coming south. That was the first time my squadron had come into real contact. We started getting mortars, RPGs and incoming machine-gun fire. I think that, for most people, was when they realised this was for real."

Whilst 7 and 16 Brigades consolidated their positions around Basrah, a stiff fight developed for An Nasiriyah and Najaf, further to the north west, between Iraqi units and US forces. This happened at the end of a 500km lightning advance by the US troops in what was probably the fastest combat move over such a distance of any land formation in military history.

Such moves require long lines of communication, which are vulnerable to ambush — as the US forces found to their cost on 23rd March near An Nasiriyah. An attack on a US supply convoy netted several prisoners. West of the city, Basrah International Airport was seized, providing a base for future operations and, eventually, for the headquarters of 1st Armoured Division.

The following day saw the noose tightening slightly around Basrah. The Black Watch and 2nd Royal Tank Regiment each suffered one battle death while clearing

Hastily reinforced former Iraqi military bases provided security for British troops as they took their first foothold in the town of Az Zubayr.

Az Zubayr. Brigadier Graham Binns subsequently explained his approach to Basrah: "In late March and early April, we conducted a number of operations using close air support to hit precise targets based on information from expert human intelligence."

Brigadier Binns used the AS90 artillery of 3rd Regiment, Royal Horse Artillery to destroy the Iraqi TV and radio networks, which was one method the regime had used to prolong the will to resist within Basrah. The rest of his troops and 16 Brigade conducted raids against the remnants of the Iraqi army and paramilitary forces in the surrounding area. Precision attacks, by ground and air, hit targets such as headquarters or meeting venues of the Ba'ath Party.

Targeting was a very sensitive matter and opposition in Basrah was — sometimes to the frustration of ground troops — tackled with restraint. At the same time, counter-attacks by Iraqi armour to the north and south of Basrah were destroyed by extremely accurate and lethal firepower. Coalition jets and helicopters worked with British artillery, armour and anti-tank guided missile systems to engage the enemy — often with first-round hits. The Lynx and Gazelle helicopters of 3 Regiment Army Air Corps flew large numbers of sorties during this phase.

Before the fighting was over, a school in Rumaylah had opened its doors to students and markets in Az Zubayr resumed business. Patrolling in Az Zubayr, Sergeant Ian Taylor, serving with The Duke of Wellington's Regiment, observed: "My main memory is the pleasure you see on the kids' faces."

By early April, British forces were patrolling in Az Zubayr wearing berets rather than helmets, projecting a more approachable stance and exploiting their unrivalled experience of winning hearts and minds in Ulster, the Balkans and Afghanistan. The confidence of junior soldiers in their own ability to communicate with strangers in a foreign culture never fails to win admirers, be they aid workers, journalists or the local population.

The AS90 self-propelled guns of the 3rd Regiment, Royal Horse Artillery were in
constant demand, laying down accurate fire on targets in and around Basrah.

Body maintenance — like that of equipment and weapons — was vital to keep the soldier
at his best. A rare opportunity to soak weary feet was a luxury to be savoured.

The flat, open marshland around Basrah International Airport was littered with the wreckage
of Iraqi tanks and armoured vehicles destroyed by the advancing coalition forces.

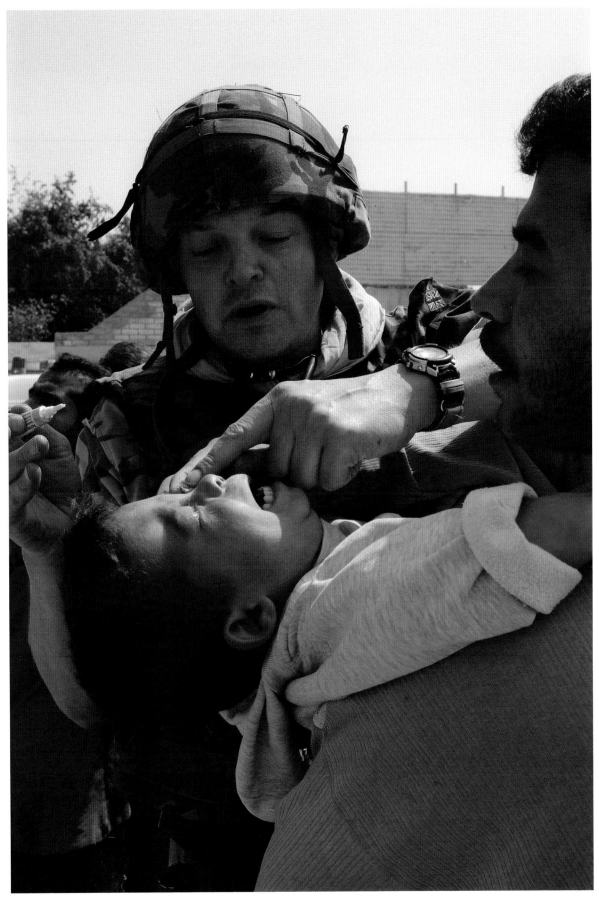

Once Az Zubayr was secured, food, water and medical aid became the next priorities. Medical facilities in the town had been limited

for a considerable time before the liberation so military doctors were inundated with requests for help from local people.

Large amounts of drugs, medical supplies and equipment had been requisitioned by the regime and stashed in Ba'ath Party strongholds. British troops in Az Zubayr worked with local doctors to set up improvised clinics and redistribute the desperately-needed supplies among them.

Water was distributed where local supplies had failed. Imam Anas, just outside Basrah, was the first village to operate a ration card system to ensure that everyone got their fair share of food and water.

The sweltering heat, heightened alert states and ever-present threat of
attack all served to turn long foot patrols into tests of endurance.

An Arabic slogan found on the wall of military base in Az Zubayr reads "Be prepared for every eventuality."

As soon as Az Zubayr was secure, soldiers from The Black Watch battlegroup exchanged their
helmets for the regiment's distinctive tam-o'-shanter in an effort to appear more approachable.

Patrols quickly gathered a fascinated, cheeky and noisy following
of children eager to practice their English or have a laugh.

Communicating with local people was vital but dialects often caused
confusion as coalition interpreters sought to make their point.

THE BATTLE FOR THE
BRIDGES

THE START OF week two of Iraq's liberation saw the 1st (UK) Division tightening its grip on Basrah. Indeed, for a while, it looked as though the campaign was settling down into two sieges — one in the south around Basrah, the other in the north as the US Army advanced to within 70km of Baghdad. It became obvious to all that the Iraqis were being forced back towards their capital quicker than they had anticipated, while their ability to command and control their forces was being rapidly eroded by coalition air assault. Fighting in the suburbs of Basrah proved grim as front lines were difficult to identify in the fog of battle. Two British tank crewmen died when their Challenger 2 was mistakenly targeted by another. However, Iraqi defenders everywhere found themselves engulfed by an air-delivered storm of steel that destroyed much and demoralised most.

On 27th March, a second front was opened up with the insertion of a US airborne brigade in the north and west of Iraq. By 28th March, Talil airbase was in US hands and was refurbished by sappers of 34 (Air Support) Field Squadron to house ground-attack aircraft and helicopters. Army and Royal Navy divers, meanwhile, had cleared Umm Qasr port of explosives and, once the Kawr Abd Allah waterway had been swept of mines, the landing ship RFA *Sir Galahad* docked with more than 700 tonnes of humanitarian aid on board. Earlier, Royal Engineers had laid a freshwater pipeline, pumping drinking water into southern Iraq.

A notable action in the fighting around Basrah happened on 28th March, when a Household Cavalry patrol from 16 Air Assault Brigade exchanged fire with

a formation of Iraqi T55 tanks. Tragically, coalition aircraft tasked to assist the tracked Scimitar armoured reconnaissance vehicles mistakenly attacked the British troops, killing one and wounding four. As helicopters arrived to evacuate the wounded, the Iraqi tanks opened fire and, after a nerve-racking wait for support, were eventually suppressed by a combination of helicopter-borne missiles, fire from the remaining Scimitars and Swingfire missiles fired from a Striker armoured vehicle. During this action, Trooper Christopher Finney rescued a wounded comrade from his blazing Scimitar, while Lance Corporal of Horse Mike Flynn directed fire at an Iraqi tank. Flynn recounted: "After 60 or 70 rounds, we put a number of scores and dents along his hull and turret. The crew abandoned their T55. However, we were still drawing fire from other positions. We managed to get a Lynx [helicopter], that had about three missiles left, returning from another mission. I fired tracers to make sure the pilot could see his target. He hit it with his second shot. All in all, I fired about 130 rounds." Flynn was awarded the Conspicuous Gallantry Cross, and Finney, aged eighteen, became the youngest soldier to win the George Cross.

Meanwhile, access to Basrah from the west was governed by five bridges over the Shatt Al Basrah waterway. "The fighting was concentrated around two of those five bridges," recalled Brigadier Graham Binns of 7th Armoured Brigade "Bridge Two, near Basrah International Airport, required the Fusiliers to secure it. They were counter-attacked by an Iraqi column and there were a number of dismounted attacks on

As the British hold on Basrah tightened, many of the city's residents, fearful of the fighting and the risks it posed, fled south to territory held by the coalition.

the bridge and fighting for a lengthy period of time." Bridge Four, further south, was the main route into Basrah. Binns continued: "We attacked Bridge Four, but it was a different kind of fighting as it was being used by civilians. The enemy would actually use civilians to provide them with cover. That bridge saw the most vicious fighting between 21st March and 6th April during the battle for Basrah."

Platoons from the Fusiliers seized both bridges, with one clearing the home bank, then the other seizing the far bank, using their Warrior infantry fighting vehicles. Overhead, shells from Challenger 2 tanks and AS90 artillery rounds pounded Iraqi machine-gun nests and armoured personnel carriers. All the while, accurate mortar fire hit the British ranks and inflicted the occasional casualty. Later on, snipers would duel with Iraqi rocket-propelled grenade teams who were trying to get close enough to attack the Challenger tanks. Days later, Black Watch soldiers witnessed these same mortars attack Iraqi civilians who were fleeing across the bridges.

On 29th March, a dawn raid by The Royal Scots Dragoon Guards and The Black Watch removed two symbols that had helped in different ways to sustain the will to resist. A statue of Saddam Hussein which had dominated a city centre park was toppled, while a 60-metre mast servicing the local TV station was felled by tank fire. Blacking out local TV and radio was a controversial decision as the facilities clearly would be needed to aid the state's recovery after the war. The decision was justified by a wane in support for the Ba'ath militia within Basrah almost immediately.

To undertake these and other missions, the battlegroups of 7th Armoured Brigade launched raids of limited duration, using a mixture of Warriors and Challengers, charging deep into the city, then withdrawing over the now-secured bridges to the west. As important, the three infantry battalions of 16 Air Assault Brigade guarded the vital oil infrastructure and dominated the approaches to Basrah from the north, shutting off access to regime hardliners, while Royal Marines from 3 Commando Brigade cleared the southern suburbs.

Although the British presence around the city was described as a siege, in fact the front line was porous. This enabled civilians to leave and some Saddam regime militants slipped away, but no more were allowed to enter. At this stage, troops from The Black

With the bridges spanning the Shatt Al Basrah waterway the only way out

of the city, human traffic flowing across them increased hour by hour.

Above and overleaf: Regular checkpoints and controls were put in place to identify and intercept any Iraqi military or militia personnel attempting to escape by posing as civilians.

Watch witnessed Iraqi mortar bombs falling on local civilians fleeing the besieged city. These weapons were fired from small courtyards and directed by observers using mobile phones. Iraqi diehards hidden in empty buildings posed similar threats with assault rifles and rocket-propelled grenades.

They all had to be removed, with minimal damage to civilians, their homes and to cultural sites. With his company targeted by accurate mortar fire, Major Paul Nansen, with The Royal Regiment of Fusiliers, remembered: "We had been attempting to call in helicopters for most of the morning. Eventually, four Cobras arrived and hovered over our beleaguered company. Controlled by the forward observer, the gunships swooped over the city, located and engaged the enemy mortar lines, relieving the pressure."

Notwithstanding the dangers of modern warfare, the 1st (UK) Armoured Division's battle area was full of hazards, as was demonstrated tragically on 1st April, when a Scimitar from The Blues and Royals overturned in an irrigation ditch. By the time that other soldiers managed to winch the vehicle upright and free the trapped crew, the gunner had drowned and the commander had sustained injuries from which he later died.

Gradually, though, the armoured raids into Basrah wore down the defenders. Soldiers remembered the 'plink-plink' of Iraqi ammunition striking the armour plates of their vehicles. The sound of gunfire came from every side as the local militia tried in vain to halt the British advance. Iraqis on rooftops fired rocket-propelled grenades or poured machine-gun fire on to the Desert Rats' vehicles but, as Captain James Moulton, of the Irish Guards, observed at the time: "The weapons they have can't really hurt us and we now know how they operate, from where, and what weapons they have." The way the Challengers and Warriors shrugged off hits from rocket-propelled grenade rounds gave their crews enormous confidence while severely demoralising their opponents.

Before approaching Basrah, fears had been voiced that urban operations would cause the sort of casualties other armies had suffered in Stalingrad or Berlin during World War Two but, nearly 60 years later, modern tactics, superb equipment and a disillusioned enemy kept British losses to a minimum. Major General Brims also had time on his side. "I'm a very patient man," he reminded the media at the time.

In an attempt to stem the flood of people leaving the city, Iraqi militia and Fedayeen threatened anyone trying to leave.
When this failed they brought mortar and small-arms fire down on their own civilians as they crossed the bridges.

This indiscriminate fire caused widespread terror and casualties among the civilians and many turned to British troops for protection. Wherever possible, British soldiers attempted to shelter civilians and give first aid to the wounded Iraqis.

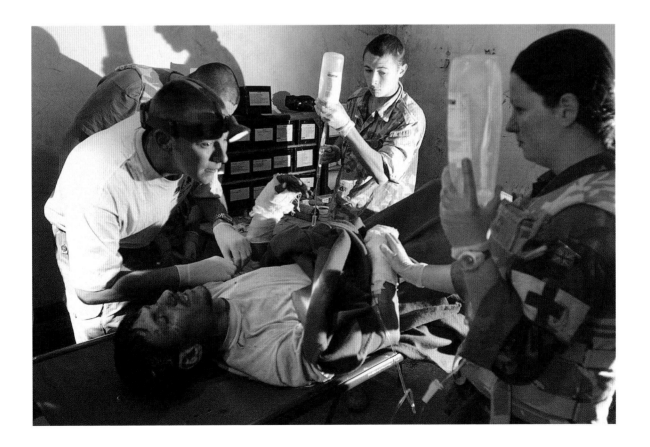

While it was occupied by the Iraqi military and Fedayeen, the Basrah Technical
College was the target for heavy artillery and mortar bombardment.

Once cleared of enemy, the college compound provided a secure base
close to the city for British troops operating on and around the bridges.

At Bridge Four we were almost always under indirect fire from the Iraqis, usually from artillery or mortars. The protection the Warriors' armour afforded and the armaments we had enabled us to operate with impunity and not to risk our soldiers' lives unnecessarily. There were occasions

when we had to dismount to fight through buildings identified as Fedayeen targets. Then we

engaged the enemy — or at least convinced them that it was a bad idea to fight against us.

MAJOR LINDSAY MACDUFF, COMPANY COMMANDER, THE BLACK WATCH

Suspected Iraqi military personnel or militia captured or surrendering were held centrally awaiting interview and processing.

Those detainees identified as prisoners of war were moved on to the coalition holding areas near Umm Qasr.

The relative security of the Basrah Technical College compound allowed troops a
respite to catch up on vital maintenance of both personal equipment and vehicles.

A soldier rarely allows himself to become separated
from his personal weapon…or his brew.

As the Headquarters of the 7th Armoured Brigade (The Desert Rats) set up on the derelict Iraqi airbase at Shaibah,
the Royal Engineers quickly fortified their position by building defensive berms between the hardened aircraft shelters.

LIBERATING
BASRAH

ON 3RD APRIL, The Queen's Royal Lancers moved forward of Bridge Two into western Basrah and set up a vehicle checkpoint. As Major Giles Harrison remembered: "Under the bridge, we came into contact with dismounted RPG teams and tanks. We destroyed one T55 and moved around to the area of the university and destroyed a second. We proved we were in control and the enemy had nothing that could touch us. We were able to sit robustly on that checkpoint despite the fact that we were under fire for almost ten hours and we controlled the ground. I think it was that action that brought forward the liberation." Harrison believes this show of force frightened off many of the regime's fanatics: "By the time we got to the Shatt Al Arab waterway, the Iraqis were already changing into civilian clothes and moving off. We had this surreal experience of watching the enemy change into their tracksuits and disappear off into the local population."

Other raids confirmed the growing British dominance in Basrah and, early on 6th April, the Divisional Commander ordered a three-pronged attack on the city. The Fusiliers attacked in the north west, The Royal Scots Dragoon Guards and Black Watch in the centre, while, to the south, 2nd Royal Tank Regiment and infantry from the Irish Guards and 1st Battalion, The Light Infantry moved in to dislodge the defenders. Before these operations, leaflets and posters were distributed and messages broadcast, testing the mood of local civilians and resistance fighters.

The Royal Scots Dragoon Guards and Irish Guards encountered some Iraqis feigning death, then 'reviving' as the Desert Rats drove near. Major Christopher Brannigan recounted: "There was a man I remember

seeing who had been lying with an RPG cradled in his arms and a cloth over his eyes. I though what an unusual position for him to be killed in. As soon as the Warriors came through, this guy jumped back up to life and fired at my tank. These attacks on the College of Literature probably took about six to eight hours by the time we finished."

As darkness descended, the raiders stayed put instead of withdrawing. The enemy attacked out of the gloom, firing into the back of an open Warrior, killing two. Elsewhere, Royal Marines seized Saddam's Basrah palace. It was a tense night — waiting, watching and wondering if the Iraqis would attack again — but thermal imaging sights gave the British an immense advantage over their opponents, who had no sophisticated night-fighting capability. The following morning, 3rd Battalion, The Parachute Regiment was ordered to advance on foot into the old town of Basrah where the streets were too narrow for Challenger and Warrior vehicles. Within two hours the Paras had secured Old Basrah without firing a shot. Said Major General Brims: "It was quite difficult because they kept getting stopped by crowds cheering them. They went through and, in fact, the opposition had left. So I ended up standing on top of a tank with the CO of 3 Para and, suddenly, there was a big crowd of Iraqis around us with happy smiling faces and I knew we had taken Basrah."

The operation, which had cost three more British lives, coincided with US operations to seize Baghdad in similar raids. While Basrah had fallen by midday on 7th April, the seizure of the Iraqi capital was confirmed on 9th April by live TV coverage of a giant bronze statue of Saddam Hussein being toppled in Al-Fardus (Paradise) Square, Baghdad.

The order to move on Basrah came quickly when it became apparent that Iraqi resistance had begun to wane. Stretched out along the road into Basrah, Warriors from the Fusiliers battlegroup waited for The Queen's Royal Lancers in their Challenger 2 tanks to clear the way ahead.

The intent for Basrah was to imagine it to be a human body. What we wanted to do was to remove the head — the head being the regime — yet keep the torso whole and the patient alive. By preserving the central nervous system, or the infrastructure, and continuing to pump the blood around the patient — the fuel, power and water — we saved the life of the patient. But at what stage should we remove the head?

BRIGADIER GRAHAM BINNS
COMMANDER, 7TH ARMOURED BRIGADE

The wreckage of Iraqi positions littered the Fusiliers battlegroup's line of advance into the city.

Destroyed by air attack, artillery fire or simply abandoned, they still had to be treated with caution.

The Iraqi Naval Academy, one of the Fusiliers battlegroup's key objectives in
the west of Basrah, was cleared of enemy by late afternoon on 6th April.

Even the most efficient razor would struggle to give a clean shave through several layers of camouflage cream.
With the risk of chemical or biological attack, shaving was essential to ensure a good seal when wearing a respirator.

A Challenger 2 from The Queen's Royal Lancers in the grounds of the Shatt Al Arab Hotel. The hotel, which overlooks the Shatt Al Arab waterway, had been the officers' mess and control tower of RAF Basrah until the British withdrawal in late 1955.

By early evening on 6th April, the Fusiliers battlegroup occupied the Shatt Al Arab Hotel.

When the Fusiliers arrived it was being stripped by looters.

The people of Basrah quickly accepted the presence
of military hardware as something quite normal.

Many of the munitions found around Basrah were in a poor state and Explosive Ordnance Disposal teams had to identify and establish the condition of finds. This surface-to-surface missile — usually ship-borne — had been placed on an improvised launcher based on an articulated lorry trailer.

Only a matter of hours after the force entered
the city, people were back on the streets.

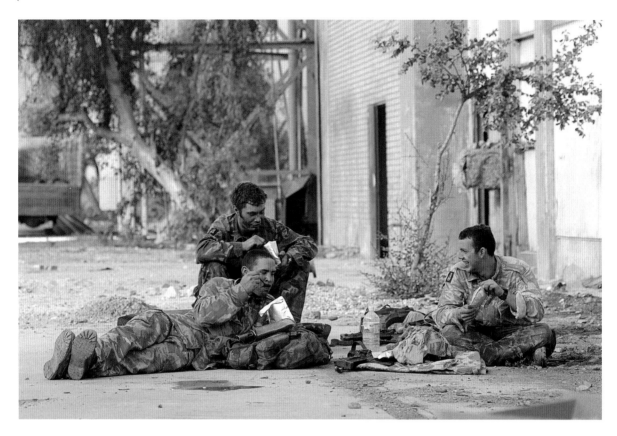

Basrah's main power station had been a key objective for the Fusiliers battlegroup. Once secured by Y Company,
1st Battalion The Royal Regiment of Fusiliers, soldiers took the opportunity to grab a quick meal.

OC Y Company, 1st Battalion, The Royal Regiment of Fusiliers briefs
the commanding officer on the situation in his company's area.

Smiling faces seemed to welcome coalition troops everywhere. Even when delayed at security
checkpoints or roadblocks, people chatted and exchanged banter with soldiers.

Basrah University offered rich pickings for looters. Where possible, troops from the Fusiliers battlegroup controlling
the compound intercepted, arrested and expelled people attempting to steal from the unguarded facilities.

Even when stationed as static sentries outside vulnerable locations, the
Challenger 2 tanks were a powerful deterrent to any would-be attacker.

With the winding alleys and streets of Old Basrah often too narrow for Challenger tanks and Warrior infantry fighting
vehicles, the 3rd Battalion, The Parachute Regiment was ordered to enter and secure this part of the city.

Firepower and manoeuvrability — the well-proven combination of armour
and infantry brought a swift end to any Iraqi military or militia resistance.

Saddam Hussein could never have imagined British Warriors would move freely about
the grounds of his Basrah palace on the banks of the Shatt Al Arab waterway.

Throughout the city more and more weapon systems and munitions were being reported to the liberating troops.

Although the munitions were often incomplete, unserviceable or improvised, every report had to be followed up.

Occupied by Iraqi military and militia, the Basrah Technical College had been the target of heavy coalition artillery and mortar fire. In the midst of the wreckage a lone flower added a defiant dash of colour.

A vital link with loved ones, free airmail letters were available to all British personnel deployed on the operation and to friends and family in the UK. The Royal Logistic Corps Postal and Courier Service and the British Forces Post Office carried tens of thousands of these letters nicknamed 'blueys'.

Initially, movement around Basrah was only possible in armoured vehicles. The only view of much of the city for many soldiers was through a small block of armoured glass.

STABILISING SOUTHERN
IRAQ

BY MID-APRIL a journalist had written "Although the capture of Basrah and Baghdad will not cause the fighting to cease, there is now light at the end of the tunnel, both for the coalition and, importantly, the Iraqi people." While military operations continued to secure Basrah and, particularly, Baghdad International Airport, British troops pushed north to link up with US forces around Al Amarah. Other military operations proceeded at a quickening pace, Kirkuk fell to Kurdish forces on 10th April and Iraqi commanders in Mosul signed a ceasefire on 11th April, while US forces entered Saddam's home town of Tikrit on 14th April.

It was obvious to most that Iraq would require substantial help to rebuild its civil infrastructure and help create the instruments of democracy once the fighting was over. Few realised just how devastated parts of the state were — not because of war damage, but through the neglect or vindictiveness of the regime, which had extensively targeted the Basrah area for reprisals after the 1991 uprisings.

A programme to raise a new Iraqi police force was managed by the Royal Military Police and within a week of the fall of Basrah, the first joint UK-Iraqi police patrols began.

The war caused relatively little damage to the country's infrastructure, although there was some looting by criminals in the immediate aftermath of Saddam's fall. Coalition forces were swift to make contact with local tribal chiefs, civic leaders and clerics in order to distribute water and food and begin the process of reconstruction. Royal Engineers teamed up with their Iraqi counterparts to get power and sewage plants, water and oil pumping stations up and running again. They ensured that 80 per cent of Basrah soon had running water — more than before the conflict — with 75 per cent of the city connected to a sewage system.

Army medical teams befriended and encouraged Iraqi doctors, dentists and nurses back to their hospitals and clinics, then protected them from looters and regime diehards. A good illustration of the immediate help British forces offered was the provision of oxygen to enable Basrah's main hospital to start life-saving operations again. Captain Naomi Bird, from 202 Field Hospital, based at Shaibah airfield, recalled: "One Iraqi boy who had lost his leg came in. Hearts will break [here] when he goes home. The kids we see are marvellous and very brave. We have two who stood on landmines, but are now mobile and getting better."

Retreating Iraqi soldiers and regime diehards abandoned numerous weapons, explosives and booby-traps, leaving explosive ordnance disposal experts many years' worth of work in making them safe. Others hid caches of weapons and ammunition which coalition troops continued to locate after the war.

In mid-April, the Umm Qasr-to-Basrah railway was reopened, courtesy of specialist Royal Engineer teams and the RLC Railway Squadron. British and Iraqi railway experts relaid track and refurbished the rolling stock, while the port of Umm Qasr began to receive shipments of overseas aid from other Gulf countries and Europe. By mid-June, after much hard work by 17 and 165 Port and Maritime Regiments, RLC, the port had been handed back to its Iraqi management.

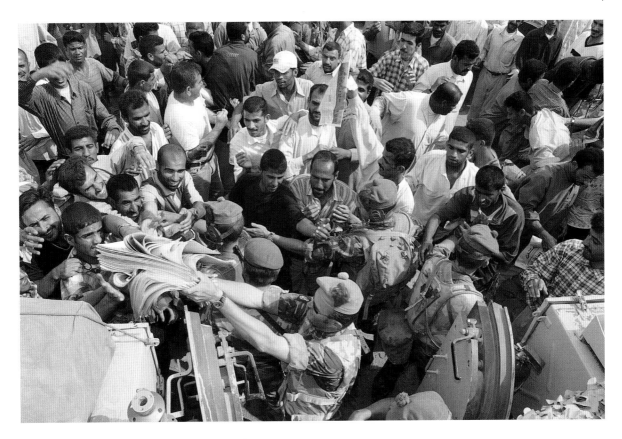

Iraqi men eagerly grab copies of the first Basrah editions of Az Zaman *Time* newspaper.
The London-based Arab language paper, distributed free by coalition forces, contained world and local news.

By July, all the 2,203 prisoners of war captured by UK forces had been processed, screened and released.

102 Logistic Brigade supplied and serviced the 1st (UK) Armoured Division throughout the war and, with the advent of peace, took responsibility for a large portion of southern Iraq. This underlines the extraordinary range of tasks today's soldiers have to tackle. In less than a month, British troops in Iraq had coped with everything from training to war-fighting to peace-building. The force in Iraq may be seen as a microcosm of the British Army, with personnel sporting almost every cap badge, and a large proportion of Territorial Army and Reservists working as a single team for a common cause.

Iraq has a wealth of natural resources, a well-educated population and is on the crossroads of major trade routes. I think it has a fantastic future. Fundamentally, the people want peace. Once they know the old regime is dead and buried they will focus on the Iraq of the future and not on the Iraq of the past.

BRIGADIER SHAUN COWLAM,
COMMANDER, 102 LOGISTIC BRIGADE

Overleaf: Scimitar armoured reconnaissance vehicles from the Blues and Royals patrol the barren landscape close to the Iranian border.

Children quickly recognised British soldiers as a source of entertainment and, on occasion, the odd sweet or unwanted packet of biscuits from their ration packs.

A soldier from the 1st Battalion, The Royal Regiment of Fusiliers meets a young visitor to the opening of the Al Maqil Health and Immunisation Clinic in Basrah. The clinic had been gutted by looters. Men from Y Company worked with staff to clean up and refit the buildings.

Soldiers from the 1st Battalion, The Black Watch monitor a breach in the wall of a Basrah police station from their Warrior armoured personnel carriers. The station was used as a base for a programme to recruit a local police force to work alongside coalition forces.

Discarded Iraqi munitions littered the city of Basrah. Often in poor and dangerous condition,
they were seen by many as a source of valuable metals to be recovered and sold as scrap.

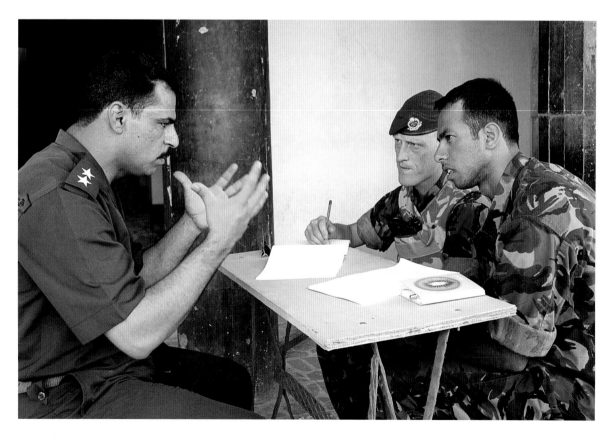

As part of the coalition plan to re-establish the region's infrastructure, former policemen
were called to report for interview and possible recruitment to a new police force.

The Warrior armoured personnel carrier served as a formidable mobile blockhouse at temporary checkpoints or fire positions in Basrah. Troops could move quickly and safely around the city and rely on its firepower and protection.

Coalition efforts to dissuade would-be salvagers of munitions were ignored, often with fatal results.

Under direction from the Coalition Provisional Authority, British troops in Basrah called former Iraqi naval personnel in
the area to a demobilisation centre to receive a one-off severance payment, formally ending their military status.

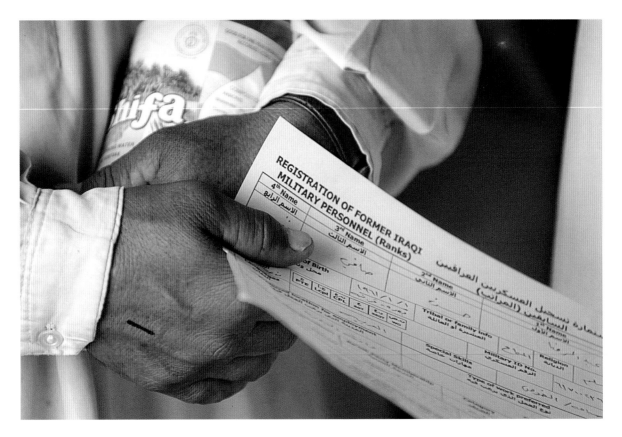

Many of the 9,200 that reported were interviewed and some 1,800 were recruited to the newly-formed Basrah River
Service, which carried out security duties on the Shatt al Arab waterway, oil installations and at key points in the region.

Mobilised reservists from the rail industry, serving with Royal Engineers Military Works Force's specialist teams, coordinated local rail workers in a programme to restore the Umm Qasr–Basrah railway, which had been badly damaged during the fighting.

Sappers from 2 (HQ) Squadron, Royal Engineers reconstruct a Bailey bridge in the village of Hamdan,
8km east of Basrah. Iraqi militia had destroyed the bridge to disrupt advancing coalition forces.

Members of the squadron scoured Iraqi military dumps to find
replacement bridge sections for those damaged when it was destroyed.

Members of the media were the constant companions of many units throughout the campaign. This team from the BBC accompanied soldiers of 3rd Regiment, Royal Horse Artillery when they deployed to intercept a gang stealing tiles from a warehouse near Basrah.

During a whirlwind visit to British units in Iraq, the Prime Minister met with Brigadier Adrian Bradshaw, the recently-appointed commander of 7th Armoured Brigade (The Desert Rats) and chatted with soldiers from many different units at the Brigade headquarters in Basrah.

By early May, having been retrained, rearmed and issued with vehicles and radios, the new police force
was taking part in regular joint patrols with and being mentored by the Royal Military Police.

English-speaking Iraqis often had a great deal
to say, as this officer from the 1st Battalion, The
Black Watch found in a village outside Basrah.

As tension reduced commanders were keen to bring their soldiers closer to the communities in which they were operating. Parking their Land Rovers and Warrior infantry fighting vehicles, J Battery, 3rd Regiment, Royal Horse Artillery patrolled their predominantly rural area on locally-hired bicycles.

As units gained the confidence of the population they were able to work with them to reinstate and rebuild facilities damaged during the fighting. The Al Maqil Health and Immunisation Clinic in Basrah, refurbished by Y Company, 1st Battalion, The Royal Regiment of Fusiliers, was a typical project.

A call home on free welfare satellite telephones was a great boost to morale. All UK personnel were issued with free phone cards that gave them 20 minutes of talk time a week.

I think it's important that we give Iraq back to the Iraqis for them to run in the way they want. It's not for us to tell them how to do things. They are a sophisticated people and they will choose whatever system suits them.

MAJOR GENERAL ROBIN BRIMS
COMMANDER, 1ST (UK) ARMOURED DIVISION

Minimi light machine-gun close to hand, a soldier from the 1st Battalion, The Black Watch
makes a free call home on one of the unit's welfare satellite telephones.

Caught in the early morning sun, a soldier from the Joint Nuclear, Biological and Chemical
Regiment patrols the lush date plantations on the banks of the Euphrates near Al Qurna.

Bombed during the first days of the war, Saddam Hussein's luxury motor yacht *Al Mansur* had been drifting slowly down the Shatt Al Arab waterway. At midday on 12th June, Royal Engineer divers examined the damage below the water line to establish the condition of the vessel. By 4.30 that afternoon it had keeled over and was lying on its starboard side in twenty feet of water.

Shaibah airfield became the site of the first Burger King and Pizza Hut outlets in southern Iraq. Mounted on articulated lorry trailers, they provided soldiers with an unexpected supplement to the rations to which they had become accustomed.

In an effort to increase local awareness of the dangers posed by the unexploded munitions and mines that littered the country, teams from the Joint Explosive Ordnance Disposal Unit visited schools and villages, talking through interpreters to children and adults alike.

The Cross of Sacrifice, Basrah War Cemetery.

IN MEMORIAM

DIED ON ACTIVE SERVICE DURING WAR-FIGHTING OPERATIONS

SERGEANT L. S. HEHIR
29 COMMANDO REGIMENT, ROYAL ARTILLERY
21ST MARCH 2003

LANCE BOMBARDIER L. C. EVANS
29 COMMANDO REGIMENT, ROYAL ARTILLERY
21ST MARCH 2003

STAFF SERGEANT S. CULLINGWORTH
33 ENGINEER REGIMENT (EOD) ROYAL ENGINEERS
23RD MARCH 2003

SAPPER L. D. ALLSOPP
33 ENGINEER REGIMENT (EOD) ROYAL ENGINEERS
23RD MARCH 2003

SERGEANT S. M. ROBERTS
2ND ROYAL TANK REGIMENT
24TH MARCH 2003

LANCE CORPORAL B. J. STEPHEN
THE BLACK WATCH
24TH MARCH 2003

CORPORAL S. J. ALLBUTT
THE QUEEN'S ROYAL LANCERS
25TH MARCH 2003

TROOPER D. J. CLARKE
THE QUEEN'S ROYAL LANCERS
25TH MARCH 2003

LANCE CORPORAL OF HORSE M. R. HULL
THE BLUES AND ROYALS
28TH MARCH 2003

LANCE CORPORAL S. A. BRIERLEY
ROYAL CORPS OF SIGNALS
30TH MARCH 2003

STAFF SERGEANT C. D. MUIR
THE ROYAL LOGISTIC CORPS
31ST MARCH 2003

LANCE CORPORAL K. R. SHEARER
THE BLUES AND ROYALS
1ST APRIL 2003

FUSILIER K. J. TURRINGTON
1ST BATTALION, THE ROYAL REGIMENT OF FUSILIERS
6TH APRIL 2003

GUARDSMAN C. MUZVURU
IRISH GUARDS
6TH APRIL 2003

LANCE CORPORAL I. K. MALONE
IRISH GUARDS
6TH APRIL 2003

LIEUTENANT A. D. TWEEDIE
THE BLUES AND ROYALS
22ND APRIL 2003

DIED ON ACTIVE SERVICE BETWEEN 29TH APRIL 2003 AND 12TH FEBRUARY 2004

LANCE CORPORAL J. McCUE
CORPS OF ROYAL ELECTRICAL AND MECHANICAL ENGINEERS
30TH APRIL 2003

PRIVATE A. J. KELLY
3RD BATTALION, THE PARACHUTE REGIMENT
6TH MAY 2003

SERGEANT S. A. HAMILTON-JEWELL
ADJUTANT GENERAL'S CORPS (ROYAL MILITARY POLICE)
24TH JUNE 2003

CORPORAL R. ASTON
ADJUTANT GENERAL'S CORPS (ROYAL MILITARY POLICE)
24TH JUNE 2003

CORPORAL S. MILLER
ADJUTANT GENERAL'S CORPS (ROYAL MILITARY POLICE)
24TH JUNE 2003

CORPORAL P. G. LONG
ADJUTANT GENERAL'S CORPS (ROYAL MILITARY POLICE)
24TH JUNE 2003

LANCE CORPORAL B. J. McG. HYDE
ADJUTANT GENERAL'S CORPS (ROYAL MILITARY POLICE)
24TH JUNE 2003

LANCE CORPORAL T. R. KEYS
ADJUTANT GENERAL'S CORPS (ROYAL MILITARY POLICE)
24TH JUNE 2003

CAPTAIN J. LINTON
40TH REGIMENT, ROYAL ARTILLERY
18TH JULY 2003

PRIVATE J. G. SMITH
52ND LOWLAND REGIMENT (VOLUNTEERS)
13TH AUGUST 2003

CAPTAIN D. M. JONES
THE QUEEN'S LANCASHIRE REGIMENT
14TH AUGUST 2003

MAJOR M. F. TITCHENER
ADJUTANT GENERAL'S CORPS (ROYAL MILITARY POLICE)
23RD AUGUST 2003

WARRANT OFFICER CLASS 2 C. WALL
ADJUTANT GENERAL'S CORPS (ROYAL MILITARY POLICE)
23RD AUGUST 2003

CORPORAL D. PRITCHARD
ADJUTANT GENERAL'S CORPS (ROYAL MILITARY POLICE)
23RD AUGUST 2003

FUSILIER R. I. J. BEESTON
52ND LOWLAND REGIMENT (VOLUNTEERS)
27TH AUGUST 2003

SERGEANT J. B. NIGHTINGALE
THE ROYAL LOGISTIC CORPS
23RD SEPTEMBER 2003

PRIVATE R. L. THOMAS
THE ROYAL REGIMENT OF WALES
6TH NOVEMBER 2003

MAJOR J. D. STENNER MC
WELSH GUARDS
1ST JANUARY 2004

SERGEANT N. PATTERSON
THE CHESHIRE REGIMENT
1ST JANUARY 2004

LANCE CORPORAL A. J. CRAW
THE ARGYLL AND SUTHERLAND HIGHLANDERS
7TH JANUARY 2004

RIFLEMAN V. C. WINDSOR
THE ROYAL GREEN JACKETS
21ST JANUARY 2004

SAPPER R. THOMSON
35 ENGINEER REGIMENT, ROYAL ENGINEERS
31ST JANUARY 2004

CORPORAL R. T. D. IVELL
CORPS OF ROYAL ELECTRICAL AND MECHANICAL ENGINEERS
12TH FEBRUARY 2004

GALLANTRY & DISTINGUISHED SERVICE AWARDS

GEORGE CROSS

TROOPER CHRISTOPHER FINNEY
THE BLUES AND ROYALS

ON 28TH MARCH, 2003, D Squadron, The Household Cavalry Regiment was probing forward along the Shatt al Arab waterway, north of Basrah, 30km ahead of the main force of 16 Air Assault Brigade. In exposed desert, their mission was to find and interdict the numerically vastly superior, and better equipped, Iraqi 6th Armoured Division.

Trooper Finney, a young armoured vehicle driver with less than a year's service, was driving the leading Scimitar vehicle of his troop, which had been at the forefront of action against enemy armour for several hours.

In the early afternoon, the two leading vehicles paused beside a levée to allow the troop leader to assess fully the situation in front. Without warning, they were engaged by a pair of coalition A10 ground attack aircraft. Both vehicles were hit and caught fire, and ammunition began exploding inside the turrets.

Finney managed to get out of his driving position and was on his way towards cover when he noticed that his gunner was trapped in the turret. He climbed on to the fiercely-burning vehicle, at the same time placing himself at risk from enemy fire, as well as fire from the A10 aircraft should they return. Despite the smoke and flames, and exploding ammunition, he managed to haul out the injured gunner, get him off the vehicle, and move him to a safer position not far away where he bandaged the wounds.

The troop officer, in the other Scimitar, had been wounded and there were no senior ranks to take control. Despite his relative inexperience, the shock of the attack and the all-too-obvious risk to himself, Finney recognised the need to inform his headquarters of the situation. He broke cover, returned to his vehicle, which was still burning, and calmly and concisely sent a lucid situation report by radio. He returned to the injured gunner and began helping him towards a Spartan vehicle of the Royal Engineers, which had moved in to assist.

At this point, Finney noticed that both the A10 aircraft were lining up for a second attack. Despite the impending danger, he continued to help his injured comrade towards the safety of the Spartan. Both aircraft fired their cannon and Finney was wounded in the buttocks and legs and the gunner in the head. Despite his wounds, Finney succeeded in getting the gunner to the waiting Spartan.

Then, seeing that the driver of the second Scimitar was still in the burning vehicle, Finney returned to rescue him as well. Despite his wounds and the continuing danger from exploding ammunition, he valiantly attempted to climb up on to the vehicle, but was beaten back by the combination of heat, smoke and exploding ammunition. He collapsed, exhausted, a short distance from the vehicle and was recovered by the crew of the Spartan.

During these attacks, and their horrifying aftermath, Finney displayed clear-headed courage and devotion to his comrades, which was out of all proportion to his age and experience. Acting with complete disregard for his own safety, even when wounded, his bravery was of the highest order throughout.

| DISTINGUISHED SERVICE ORDER | CONSPICUOUS GALLANTRY CROSS | MILITARY CROSS | DISTINGUISHED FLYING CROSS | QUEEN'S GALLANTRY MEDAL (REVERSE) | MENTION IN DESPATCHES |

DISTINGUISHED SERVICE ORDER

BRIGADIER GRAHAM JOHN BINNS CBE MC
LATE THE PRINCE OF WALES'S OWN REGIMENT OF YORKSHIRE

**MAJOR GENERAL
ROBIN VAUGHAN BRIMS CBE**
LATE THE LIGHT INFANTRY

**LIEUTENANT COLONEL
MICHAEL LAWRENCE RIDDELL-WEBSTER**
THE BLACK WATCH

MAJOR RICHARD COWAN TAYLOR
THE LIFE GUARDS

CONSPICUOUS GALLANTRY CROSS

LANCE CORPORAL OF HORSE MICHAEL JOHN FLYNN
THE BLUES AND ROYALS

MILITARY CROSS

SERGEANT NATHAN LEWIS BELL
THE PARACHUTE REGIMENT

GUARDSMAN ANTON LIAM BRANCHFLOWER
IRISH GUARDS

CAPTAIN CHARLES OLIVER CAMPBELL
THE ROYAL REGIMENT OF FUSILIERS

SERGEANT CRAIG GEORGE JAMES COMBER
CORPS OF ROYAL ELECTRICAL AND MECHANICAL ENGINEERS

LIEUTENANT SIMON THOMAS FAREBROTHER
THE QUEEN'S DRAGOON GUARDS

LIEUTENANT CHRISTOPHER ASHLEY HEAD
THE ROYAL REGIMENT OF FUSILIERS

SERGEANT MARK JACK HELEY
CORPS OF ROYAL ENGINEERS

CAPTAIN GRANT INGLETON
ROYAL REGIMENT OF ARTILLERY

**STAFF SERGEANT
RICHARD PETER THOMAS JOHNSON**
CORPS OF ROYAL ENGINEERS

LANCE CORPORAL PETER WILLIAM LAING
THE BLACK WATCH

LIEUTENANT DANIEL CHARLES MORGAN O'CONNELL
IRISH GUARDS

**LIEUTENANT
THOMAS PETER ALGAR ORDE-POWLETT**
IRISH GUARDS

LIEUTENANT TOBY CHRISTIAN RIDER
CORPS OF ROYAL ENGINEERS

CORPORAL JOHN WILLIAM RANDOLPH ROSE
THE BLACK WATCH

MAJOR HENRY FRANCIS AUSTIN SUGDEN
THE QUEEN'S DRAGOON GUARDS

DISTINGUISHED FLYING CROSS

**WARRANT OFFICER CLASS 2
RUPERT ST JOHN HARDINGTON BANFIELD**
ARMY AIR CORPS

CAPTAIN RICHARD TIMOTHY CUTHILL
ARMY AIR CORPS

QUEEN'S GALLANTRY MEDAL

CAPTAIN TIMOTHY ROBERT GOULD
ROYAL LOGISTIC CORPS

STAFF SERGEANT ANDREW WILLIAM SINDALL
CORPS OF ROYAL ENGINEERS

POSTHUMOUS MENTION IN DESPATCHES

LANCE CORPORAL BARRY JAMES STEPHEN
THE BLACK WATCH

FUSILIER KELAN JOHN TURRINGTON
THE ROYAL REGIMENT OF FUSILIERS

HER MAJESTY THE QUEEN APPROVED AN ADDITIONAL 368 AWARDS
FOR GALLANTRY AND DISTINGUISHED SERVICE TO MEMBERS OF THE ARMED SERVICES.

OPERATION TELIC
ORDER OF BATTLE — JANUARY-JUNE 2003

HEADQUARTERS

1st (UK) Armoured Division HQ
and Signal Regiment

*3rd (UK) Armoured Division HQ
and Signal Regiment*

4th Armoured Brigade HQ and Signal Squadron

7th Armoured Brigade HQ
and Signal Squadron

16 Air Assault Brigade HQ
and Signal Squadron

102 Logistic Brigade HQ
and Signal Squadron

HOUSEHOLD CAVALRY
AND ROYAL ARMOURED CORPS

The Household Cavalry Regiment

1st The Queen's Dragoon Guards

The Royal Scots Dragoon Guards

The Queen's Royal Lancers

1st Royal Tank Regiment
(Joint NBC Regiment)

2nd Royal Tank Regiment

The Royal Yeomanry

ROYAL HORSE ARTILLERY

3rd Regiment, Royal Horse Artillery

7th Parachute Regiment,
Royal Horse Artillery

ROYAL REGIMENT OF ARTILLERY

5th Regiment, Royal Artillery

12th Regiment, Royal Artillery

26th Regiment, Royal Artillery

29 Commando Regiment, Royal Artillery

32nd Regiment, Royal Artillery

40th Regiment, Royal Artillery

47th Regiment, Royal Artillery

395 Air Defence Troop (Volunteers)

CORPS OF ROYAL ENGINEERS

12 (Air Support) Engineer Brigade HQ

23 Engineer Regiment

28 Engineer Regiment

32 Engineer Regiment

*33 Engineer Regiment
(Explosive Ordnance Disposal)*

36 Engineer Regiment

38 Engineer Regiment

39 Engineer Regiment (Airfield Support)

42 Engineer Regiment (Geo)

*59 (Independent) Commando Regiment,
Royal Engineers*

Military Works Force
62 and 63 Specialist Teams

Military Works Force 64 Specialist Team

Civil Affairs Group

412 Amphibious Troop,
Royal Engineers (Volunteers)

ROYAL CORPS OF SIGNALS

2 Signal Regiment

10 Signal Regiment

14 Signal Regiment

21 Signal Regiment

30 Signal Regiment

Royal Signals System Support Team

Army Tactical Computer System
Support Team

REGIMENT OF FOOT GUARDS

1st Battalion, Irish Guards

INFANTRY

1st Battalion, The Royal Regiment of Fusiliers

1st Battalion, The Light Infantry

1st Battalion, The Royal Irish Regiment

1st Battalion,
The Duke of Wellington's Regiment

1st Battalion, The Black Watch
(Royal Highland Regiment)

1st Battalion, The Parachute Regiment

3rd Battalion, The Parachute Regiment

*4th Battalion The Parachute Regiment
(Volunteers)*

ARMY AIR CORPS

3 Regiment, Army Air Corps

ROYAL LOGISTIC CORPS

1 General Support Regiment,
Royal Logistic Corps

2 Close Support Regiment,
Royal Logistic Corps

6 Supply Regiment, Royal Logistic Corps

7 Transport Regiment, Royal Logistic Corps

8 Transport Regiment, Royal Logistic Corps

9 Supply Regiment, Royal Logistic Corps

10 Transport Regiment, Royal Logistic Corps

*11 Explosive Ordnance Disposal Regiment,
Royal Logistic Corps*

*13 Air Assault Support Regiment,
Royal Logistic Corps*

17 Port and Maritime Regiment,
Royal Logistic Corps

23 Pioneer Regiment, Royal Logistic Corps

24 Regiment, Royal Logistic Corps

27 Transport Regiment, Royal Logistic Corps

29 Regiment, Royal Logistic Corps

*132 Aviation Supply Squadron,
Royal Logistic Corps*

165 Port and Maritime Regiment,
Royal Logistic Corps (Volunteers)

*166 Supply Regiment,
Royal Logistic Corps (Volunteers)*

496 Logistic Liaison Unit,
Movement Support Group,
Royal Logistic Corps (Volunteers)

101 Military Working Dogs

Commando Logistic Regiment

ROYAL ARMY MEDICAL CORPS

1 Close Support Medical Regiment

4 General Support Medical Regiment

5 General Support Medical Regiment

16 Close Support Medical Regiment

33 Field Hospital

34 Field Hospital

202 Field Hospital (Volunteers)

ROYAL ELECTRICAL AND
MECHANICAL ENGINEERS

2nd Battalion,
Royal Electrical and Mechanical Engineers

3rd Battalion,
Royal Electrical and Mechanical Engineers

7 Air Assault Battalion,
Royal Electrical and Mechanical Engineers

ROYAL MILITARY POLICE

1 Regiment, Royal Military Police

5 Regiment, Royal Military Police

156 Provost Company, Royal Military Police

INTELLIGENCE CORPS

1st Military Intelligence Brigade

1 Military Intelligence Battalion

2 Military Intelligence Battalion

3 Military Intelligence Battalion (Volunteers)

4 Military Intelligence Battalion

*15 (United Kingdom)
Psychological Operations Group*

MEDIA OPERATIONS

Media Operations Group (Volunteers)

DEFENCE FIRE SERVICE

Service Defence Fire Service (Army)

[UNITS WHICH DID NOT DEPLOY IN THEIR ENTIRETY ARE SHOWN IN ITALICS]